101 FUN RIDDLES AND ANAGRAMS

For Kids!

By M.J. Farrell

101 Fun Riddles and Anagrams for Kids. Written and published by M.J. Farrell.

Copyright 2017 M.J. Farrell. All rights reserved. No portion of this book may be reproduced in any form without permission from the author and publisher, except as permitted by U.S. copyright law. For permissions contact the author at mjfarrell75@gmail.com.

FUN RIDDLES..1

    What Am I?...1

    These Are a Bit Trickier!....................5

    What Is It?..7

    Give Up Yet? Here Are The Answers to The Riddles!....................10

ANAGRAMS..13

    Give Up Yet? Here Are The Answers to The Riddles!....................20

FUN RIDDLES

What Am I?

1. You can't see or touch me, but I can be broken very easily. What am I?

2. I don't have arms or legs and you can't see me; but I am easy to catch. What am I?

3. You cannot walk away without leaving me behind; and you cannot take me with you when you walk away. What am I?

4. I start out tall and bright, but as time passes by I get smaller and smaller. What am I?

5. I will always arrive, but I can never come today. What am I?

6. I have eighty-eight keys, but I can never open any doors. What am I?

7. I have roads but no cars; I have rivers but no fish; I have cities and town but no people. What am I?

8. I am flat and can travel all over the world even though I just stay in one corner. What am I?

9. You will find me in America. I have four eyes, but can't see. What am I?

10. I can't get wetter no matter how much rain falls on me. What am I?

11. I go around in circles, but always straight ahead. What am I?

12. These two things can always see what the other sees, but can never see each other? What are they?

13. I can only come down but I can never go up. What am I?

14. I have a neck but no head, and I am easy to break. What am I?

15. I have a thumb and four fingers but I am not alive? What am I?

16. I am hot. I am bright. Don't look straight at me. I disappear in the night. What am I?

17. I will still be hot even if you put me in the refrigerator. What am I?

18. I am tiny and have an eye, but cannot see. What am I?

19. I have a head and tail but no body. What am I?

20. I follow you everywhere and I weigh nothing. What am I?

HOW DO YOU WRITE A RIDDLE?

RIDDLES CAN BE ABOUT ANYTHING! RIDDLES CAN BE ABOUT ANIMALS OR OBJECTS. A RIDDLE CAN BE FUNNY OR IT CAN RHYME. THERE ARE NO RULES!

21. You look at me and I look back at you. You raise your right hand and I raise my left. What am I?

These are a Bit Trickier!

22. How many oranges grow on a tree?

23. You can hold this without using your hands or arms.

24. When this is clean, it is black; but the dirtier it gets, the whiter it becomes.

25. How many apples can you eat on an empty stomach?

26. How many months in the year have twenty-eight days?

27. Which word is spelled wrong in every dictionary?

28. Where is the only place in the world where today comes before yesterday?

29. If you have one of these, you don't share it. If you share it, you will no longer have it. What is it?

30. What becomes wetter the more it dries?

31. What has two hands but can never clap?

32. These are two things that you can never have at breakfast. What are they?

What is It?

33. This always has to be broken before you can use it. What is it?

34. This can up and down, but never moves. What is it?

35. This belongs to you, but is used all the time by others. What is it?

36. This is something that can't be touched or smelt; and can only be held by two or more people. What is it?

37. This has one head, one foot and four legs. What is it?

38. The more there is of this, the less you will see. What is it?

39. This has many teeth but cannot eat. What is it?

40. This can run but never walks, it has a mouth but never eats, it has a bed but never sleeps? What is it?

INTERESTING FACT:

THE OLDEST KNOWN RIDDLE DATES BACK TO ANCIENT EGYPT, AROUND 2,500 YEARS AGO!

41. This has skin and many eyes, yet cannot see. What is it?

42. You can always count of these to solve a math problem. What are they?

43. This increases as time passes but never decreases. What is it?

44. This is full of holes, but can still hold water. What is it?

45. This type of building can be just one floor, but still have many stories. What is it?

46. This is black when you buy it, red when you use it, and gray when you throw it away. What is it?

GIVE UP YET? HERE ARE THE ANSWERS TO THE RIDDLES!

1. Silence
2. A cold
3. Foot Steps
4. A candle
5. Tomorrow
6. A piano
7. A map
8. A postage stamp
9. Mississippi
10. Water
11. A wheel
12. Your eyes
13. Rain
14. A bottle
15. A glove
16. The sun

17. A pepper

18. A needle

19. A coin

20. Your shadow

21. A mirror

22. All of them!

23. Your breath

24. Chalkboard or blackboard

25. Only one apple because after that, your stomach is no longer empty.

26. All of them!

27. Wrong

28. A dictionary

29. A secret

30. A Towel

31. A clock

32. Lunch and dinner

33. An egg

34. The temperature

35. Your name

36. A conversation

37. A bed

38. Darkness

39. A comb

40. A River

41. A Potato

42. Your fingers

43. Your age

44. A sponge

45. A library

46. Charcoal

ANAGRAMS!

What is an Anagram?

You pronounce it as "AN-uh-gram" and it is simply a word that you can form by rearranging the letters of another word.

Sounds simple enough right? Well, let's see if you can figure out these anagrams!

1. ACTS

2. ADD

3. AFIELD

4. APE

5. ARE

6. MARS

7. ART

8. ATE

9. BELOW

10. BRUSH

11. CALM

12. CANOE

13. CARE

14. CAUSE

15. CHIN

16. CLOUD

17. ONE

18. CORK

19. COSMIC

20. DAIRY

> **How Do You Solve an Anagram?**
>
> If you get stuck, just write the word backwards on a piece of paper, or write in in a circle! Why do this? Well, it will take your mind off the original word and its meaning.

21. DARE

22. DISK

23. DUSTY

24. EAST

25. HOSE

26. HOW

27. SINK

28. KISS

29. LAMP

30. LIMES

31. LISTEN

32. LUMP

33. MEAT

34. METEOR

35. NAILS

36. NIGHT

37. RINSE

38. WEATHER

39. BELOW

40. RITE

41. RING

42. CARE

43. SKIN

44. LOOP

45. PEACH

46. WEST

47. COLA

> Here is another tip to solve anagrams: always use capital letters.
>
> For some reason it helps you figure them out!

48. PLAYERS

49. MELON

50. NORTH

51. EASTERN

52. OWL

53. NIGHT

54. LEAF

55. COAT

GIVE UP YET? HERE ARE THE ANSWERS TO THE ANAGRAMS!

1. CATS or CAST

2. DADS

3. FAILED

4. PEA

5. EAR

6. ARMS

7. RAT or TAR

8. EAT or TEA

9. ELBOW

10. SHRUB

11. CLAM

12. OCEAN

13. RACE

14. SAUCE

15. INCH

16. COULD

17. ONCE

18. ROCK

19. COMICS

20. DIARY

21. DEAR or READ

22. KIDS or SKID

23. STUDY

24. EATS or SEAT

25. HOSE

26. WHO

27. SKIN

28. SKIS

29. PALM

30. MILES or SMILE

31. SILENT

32. PLUM

33. TEAM

34. REMOTE

35. SNAIL

36. THINGS

37. SIREN

38. WREATH

39. NILE

40. TIRE

41. GRIN

42. RACE

43. SINK

44. POOL

45. CHEAP

46. STEW

47. COAL

48. PARSLEY

49. LEMON

50. THORN

51. NEAREST

52. LOW

53. THING

54. FLEA

55. TACO

I truly hope you enjoyed this book as much as I have writing it. Just remember, the best part of sharing these riddles and anagrams with your kids is not only exercising their minds, but also spending time together!

M.J. Farrell

Printed in Great Britain
by Amazon

83346666R00016